Fast Italian

The Flavor of Italy—in a Flash!

> Author: Margit Proebst | Photos: Michael Boyny

Contents

Theory

The Recipes

Appendix

Presto, Prestissimo, …

Italy is a dream vacation-land whose cuisine can leave you speechless. You're about to learn how easy it is to add a little Mediterranean flair to your own everyday life. All you need are a few fresh ingredients, a laid-back attitude, and, above all, just a little bit of time. Quick and delicious Italian dishes can be prepared in a flash and then easily combined to make a meal, leaving you all the more time to enjoy yourself with your loved ones. And that's really what the "dolce vita all'italiana" is all about.

The Eight Highlights of Italian Cuisine

Tomatoes: Aromatic tomatoes are one of life's greatest pleasures. (Out of season, you're better off using peeled, canned tomatoes and tomato paste for soups and sauces.) But for fresh combinations such as caprese (tomatoes, mozzarella, basil), you have a choice of beefsteak tomatoes, vine-ripened, plum, cherry, and many others. Also, sun-dried tomatoes (in oil or reconstituted) work well used as an antipasto or in pasta sauces.

Pasta: Spaghetti, tagliatelle, penne, linguine: Italian pasta, made from durum wheat (grano duro), comes in numerous shapes and can be served with myriad sauces for delicious appetizers and entrées. Additionally, noodles made with egg or other ingredients such as saffron, spinach, tomatoes, mushrooms, and squid ink are worth pursuing — look for fresh, and cook them "al dente," meaning "firm to the teeth."

Herbs: Fresh herbs such as basil, rosemary, thyme, and sage give Italian cuisine its unmistakable aroma and appeal. Thanks to their many vitamins and trace minerals, these herbs are also very good for you. Use them liberally! Arugula is taking European kitchens by storm — and rightly so — since this spicy, piquant herb not only peps up salads but also tastes great on crostini and pizza, and in pasta dishes.

Pine nuts: Pine nuts are the seeds of pine trees carefully removed from pine cones, which explains their high price. A handful in a salad or pesto (page 11) turns a simple dish into a feast. Toasting them until golden-brown is the best way to highlight their buttery and nutty flavor. And like walnuts, they're rich in essential unsaturated fatty acids.

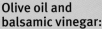

Olive oil and balsamic vinegar:

Each Italian region has its own olive oil, each one unique due to differing soil and climate. Be sure to use extra virgin olive oil on salads and for marinating antipasti. Balsamic vinegar is also a must for gourmets. Aged in oak casks for months, the higher quality balsamics take many years to mature. Of these, only a small amount is needed to give salads or sauces that typically smooth, delicately acidic aroma.

Cheese:

The most famous cheeses are Gorgonzola, a creamy blue; Taleggio, tangy and soft; Scamorza, smoky, hard, and made from cow's milk; and Pecorino, made from goat's milk (mild or strong, depending on the age and region). And who could forget Parmesan? Try it freshly grated on pasta, shaved on salad, or solo with red wine. Ricotta and mascarpone are fresh Italian cheeses, ideal for desserts.

Ham, bresàola, and sausages:

Air-dried Parma ham, mortadella, and salami are also available outside Italy. Bresàola (a smoked, air-dried specialty beef) is harder to find yet delicious when shaved in paper-thin slices and served on toasted bread or in salads. A little ham and salami, a few olives, and some marinated artichoke hearts make a quick antipasti platter.

Ciabatta and focaccia:

Ciabatta is a crispy white bread gaining in popularity outside of Italy; focaccia is flatbread often topped with herbs and olive oil (that can also be used as a side dish). Additionally, here's how to make crostini from day-old bread: Toast slices until golden, add a flavorful spread, and serve with an aperitif.

5

Italian Menus
Putting Them Together

In real life, people seldom find the time or energy to cook extensive meals. Nevertheless, a little "italianità" can't hurt. How about serving a salad as an appetizer, pasta as a main dish, and fresh seasonal fruits for dessert? Round off this little menu with an espresso and some store-bought amarettino (almond cookies). You can expand it for holidays and guests as follows: Reduce the amount of pasta or risotto and serve a meat or fish dish; plus, add a sweet dessert along with the fruit (and maybe even a cheese course). On special occasions, offer crostini with an aperitif. The first course can be cold antipasti, followed by a small serving of pasta or risotto. As the main dish, serve a little meat or fish with a vegetable or potato side dish. Finish with a sweet dessert and/or cheese followed by an espresso drink and an after-dinner liqueur.

For detailed menu suggestions that include dishes from this book, see pages 58 and 59. Now just put on a Lucio Dalla or Gianna Nannini CD, and there's nothing to keep you from entering into a mini-vacation…

Aperitif

Nobody says "no" to tasty crostini.
Served with a glass of Prosecco, they're
a promising warm-up to a traditional
Italian meal.

∧ 1

∨ 3 ## Finale

Finishing up with an espresso (simply
called "caffè" in Italian) and a little
Grappa helps aid in digestion.

Fresh Italian bread

2

Crusty bread never goes out of
style—whether with antipasti,
used for crostini, or for dipping
in a sauce.

The Right Drinks

Aperitifs: To pass the time before a meal and prepare the stomach for the delights to come, offer your guests an aperitif. This can be a Campari (with soda or orange juice), or perhaps Cynar on the rocks or mixed with mineral water. If you prefer fruity aperitifs, choose a "Bellini"—a combination of peach purée and Prosecco.

Prosecco: The Prosecco grape is primarily cultivated in Veneto and Friuli and usually, but not always, turned into a sparkling wine (there is also a still variety). In recent years, Prosecco has become a favorite drink outside of Italy, equally suitable for a "toast" at the office or as an aperitif before a festive meal.

Wine: Italy is a typical wine country with extensive cultivation and a mild, warm climate that produces many fine vintages. A selection of recipes in this book include wine recommendations, but you can also experiment for yourself to discover your own favorites. In Italy, wine is consumed only with meals—an exemplary custom, as wine consumed in moderation is beneficial for your health.

Dessert wines: The most famous is Marsala, available in both dry (secco) and semisweet (dolce) versions. It pairs well with desserts but is also used in sweet dishes and sauces. Another well-loved dessert wine is Vin Santo ("sacred wine"), often served after a meal in small glasses like a liqueur.

After-dinner liqueurs: Italians also welcome brandy as a digestif. Choose an Amaro, Grappa, or a brandy such as Vecchia Romagna. They are a worthy finish to a multi-course meal.

Non-alcoholic: In Italy, every meal is accompanied by a jug of fresh cold water on the table. If you order mineral water in a restaurant, you need to specify acqua gassata (carbonated) or acqua naturale (uncarbonated). The delicious fruit juices served in small glass bottles, such as succo di albicocca (apricot juice) and succo di pera (pear juice), aren't just for children. Fresh-squeezed juice is called "spremuta."

Coffee: Italian coffee is dark-roasted, which gives it a pleasant, tangy flavor and also makes it very digestible. Italians follow a meal with an espresso, which they simply call "caffè." An "authentic" Italian household always has an espresso machine. Whether it's a small aluminum macchinetta or a fancy, pressure-operated professional machine with a spout for foaming milk depends on the family's preferences and budget.

Cappuccino, etc.: If you like a shot of milk in your coffee, try a caffè macchiato (Italian for "stained"). Cappuccino (espresso with foamed milk), caffè latte (milk coffee), and latte macchiato (lots of milk with a little coffee) are favorites for breakfast and any other occasion throughout the day. In addition, caffè with a shot of Grappa is a caffè corretto.

Basic Recipe

Everybody loves vegetable antipasti such as sautéed oyster mushrooms, zucchini, or eggplant—all of which are quick to prepare. Since they keep in the refrigerator for days, it's worth making extra. This way, you'll readily have a delicious vegetarian appetizer on hand.

Mushroom Antipasti

SERVES 4:

➤ 1 lb oyster mushrooms
$^1/_3$ cup olive oil
2 cloves garlic
$^1/_2$ cup fresh parsley sprigs
$^1/_4$ cup fresh lemon juice
Salt and pepper

TIP

Vegetable Antipasti

You can use the same recipe to prepare zucchini and eggplant slices or bell pepper pieces. Try different seasonings each time such as thyme, sage, or oregano, according to your inclination.

> **1** *Remove thick stems from oyster mushrooms. Leave small mushrooms whole and cut up large mushrooms.*

> **2** *Sauté mushrooms over medium-high heat in 4 tbs olive oil until golden-brown. Add garlic squeezed through a press, chopped parsley, salt, and pepper to taste.*

> **3** *Transfer to a bowl and when lukewarm, drizzle with fresh lemon juice and remaining olive oil as desired.*

Basic Pesto Recipe

Pesto is a treasured paste made from herbs, Parmesan, toasted pine nuts, garlic, and olive oil. It's excellent as a spread on bruschetta and crostini, as a sauce for pasta and gnocchi, and as a filling for rolled pasta or meats (involtini). To prepare pesto, either crush all the ingredients finely in a mortar and pestle or process using a blender, hand blender, or food processor. Add olive oil (2 tbs for crostini and involtini, and up to $1/3$ cup for a pasta or gnocchi sauce). Store in a clean screw-top jar and cover the surface with more olive oil. In this manner, pesto will keep refrigerated for weeks and can be used to prepare great dishes with short notice. When using pesto with pasta, add a few tablespoons of the pasta cooking water while tossing together.

The recipes on the right each yield about enough for 1 lb of pasta (or enough for 20 crostini or 4–6 involtini).

Basil Pesto

➤ 1 cups fresh basil sprigs
 $1/3$ cup toasted pine nuts
 $1^1/2$ oz freshly grated Parmesan
 1 clove garlic
 Olive oil
 Salt and pepper

Arugula Pesto

➤ 2 cups arugula leaves
 $1/3$ cup toasted pine nuts
 $1^1/2$ oz freshly grated Parmesan
 Olive oil
 1 clove garlic
 Salt and pepper

Tomato Pesto

➤ 10 sun-dried tomatoes (in oil; drained)
 $1/3$ cup toasted pine nuts
 $1^1/2$ oz freshly grated Parmesan
 1 clove garlic
 $1/4$ to $1/2$ tsp crushed red pepper flakes
 Olive oil | Salt

Hazelnut Pesto

➤ $3/4$ cup toasted, skinned hazelnuts
 $1^1/2$ oz freshly grated Parmesan
 1 clove garlic
 Olive oil
 Salt and pepper

11

Antipasti: Appetizers and Salads

A successful opener can turn a simple meal into a memorable dining experience. Whether served as a snack, along with an aperitif, or as an official appetizer...whether the first course of an opulent menu or the start to a light summer dinner, Italian antipasti are extremely difficult to resist.

Quick Recipes

Tomatoes with Mozzarella
Caprese

SERVES 4:

➤ 4 ripe beefsteak tomatoes (1 to 1$^{1}/_{2}$ lbs) | $^{1}/_{2}$ lb fresh mozzarella (di bufala or boconccini) | 1 cup fresh basil sprigs | $^{1}/_{3}$ cup extra virgin olive oil | Salt and pepper

1 | Rinse tomatoes and slice. Slice fresh mozzarella. Rinse basil and pat dry.

2 | Arrange overlapping slices of tomato and fresh mozzarella on four plates and sprinkle with basil leaves. Season with salt and pepper, and drizzle with extra virgin olive oil.

Melon and Ham
Prosciutto e melone

SERVES 4:

➤ 1 honeydew melon | 12 slices prosciutto (about $^{1}/_{3}$ lb) | 12 wooden toothpicks

1 | Cut melon into 12 wedges, remove seeds and cut fruit away from rind. Arrange 3 melon wedges on each plate.

2 | Twist prosciutto slices loosely into "sails" and secure with toothpicks to melon "boats."

Inexpensive

Tomato-Basil Toast
Bruschetta ai pomodori

SERVES 4:
- 4 ripe beefsteak tomatoes (about 1 to 1$1/4$ lbs)
  $1/2$ cup fresh basil sprigs
  $1/3$ cup extra virgin olive oil
  1 clove garlic
  4 large slices Italian bread ($1/2$ inch thick)
  Salt and pepper

- Prep time: 20 minutes
- Calories per serving: About 250

1 | Briefly submerge tomatoes in boiling water; peel, halve crosswise, and remove seeds. Dice tomatoes finely and season with salt and pepper. Rinse basil, cut leaves into fine strips, and mix with diced tomatoes.

2 | Peel garlic, squeeze through a press, and mix with olive oil. Brush garlic oil onto bread slices. Toast bread on both sides until crispy (see tip). Drizzle a little of the garlic oil onto the tomato-basil mixture. While still warm, top with tomato-basil mixture and enjoy!

- Beverage: Light red wine or beer

Easy | For Company

Crostini with Bresàola
Crostini con bresàola

SERVES 4:
- $1/2$ cup fresh basil sprigs
  $3 1/2$ oz ricotta
  6 cherry tomatoes
  12 slices baguette
  12 slices bresàola (may substitute 6 slices prosciutto, halved)
  2 tbs toasted pine nuts
  Salt and pepper

- Prep time: 20 minutes
- Calories per serving: About 420

1 | Rinse basil. Pluck off 12 nice leaves and set aside for garnish. Cut remaining leaves into fine strips and mix with ricotta. Season to taste with salt and pepper. Rinse cherry tomatoes and halve.

2 | Toast baguette slices until golden-brown (see tip). While still warm, spread with ricotta mixture. Twist each cured ham slice into a rosette and place on top. Garnish each slice with 1 basil leaf, a few toasted pine nuts, and a half cherry tomato; serve at once.

- Beverage: Prosecco

TIPS
- The pestos on page 11 are also suitable spreads for crostini. The following combinations are especially delicious:

  Arugula pesto and prosciutto di Parma

  Basil pesto and smoked salmon

  Hazelnut pesto and smoked turkey breast

  Tomato pesto and sautéed shrimp

- Toast bread either in a toaster or under the oven broiler.

Photo top: **Tomato-Basil Toast**   Photo bottom: **Crostini with Bresàola**

For Company | Vegetarian

Eggplant Rolls
Involtini di melanzane

MAKES 12 ROLLS:

- ➤ 2 eggplant (about 1 to 1^1/$_4$ lbs)
- 1 clove garlic
- ^{1}/$_3$ cup olive oil
- 2 sprigs thyme
- ^{1}/$_2$ cup pitted green olives (imported type; no pimentos)
- ^{1}/$_3$ cup ground almonds
- 1 tsp honey
- 7 oz ricotta salata (semi-hard; may substitute mild Feta)
- Salt and pepper
- Wooden toothpicks

🕐 Prep time (not including refrigeration): 40 minutes

➤ Calories per serving: About 90

1 | Rinse eggplant and cut lengthwise into ^{1}/$_4$-inch thick slices. Sprinkle generously with salt and let stand for 5 minutes to draw out water. Preheat oven to 375°F. Peel garlic, squeeze through a press, and mix with olive oil. Chop thyme leaves (stripped from stem) coarsely.

2 | Squeeze out eggplant, pat dry and lay out on a greased baking sheet. Brush with garlic-oil mixture and broil in the oven for 8–10 minutes or until golden-brown on both sides. Remove, season with salt and pepper, and sprinkle with thyme; let cool.

3 | Set aside 12 olives (for optional garnish) and purée remaining olives together with almonds, honey, salt, and pepper. Cut ricotta salata into matchstick strips. Spread olive-almond mixture on 12 eggplant slices and top with ricotta salata strips. Roll up slices and secure each roll with 1 toothpick and 1 olive if desired.

TIP

Grilled eggplant, marinated with a little fresh lemon juice and olive oil, enhances any antipasti buffet, even without a filling. You can also chop grilled or roasted eggplant and blend it with the olive-almond mixture for use as a spread.

Also Delicious Cold

Fennel Gratin
Finocchi gratinati

SERVES 4:

- ➤ 4 young fennel bulbs
- 1 lemon
- 2 oz freshly grated Parmesan
- 2 oz (4 tbs) butter
- Nutmeg
- Salt and pepper

🕐 Prep time: 35 minutes

➤ Calories per serving: About 170

1 | Bring salted water to a boil. Rinse fennel, cut bulbs into quarters, and set aside leafy fronds. Rinse lemon, pat dry, and cut into thick slices. Simmer fennel and lemon slices for 10–12 minutes until tender; drain. Preheat oven to 425°F.

2 | Chop some of the fennel fronds and mix with Parmesan. Grease a gratin or baking dish with butter and fill with fennel bulbs. Season with pepper, sprinkle with Parmesan mixture, and top with remaining butter cut into bits. Bake (middle rack) until tops are golden.

For Gourmets

Sautéed Trevisano
Trevisano trifolato

SERVES 4:

➤ 4 heads trevisano (may substitute red endive or any chicory)
1/3 cup olive oil
2 tbs pine nuts
2 tbs balsamic vinegar
1 tbs honey
Salt and pepper

🕐 Prep time: 15 minutes
➤ Calories per serving: About 195

1 │ Rinse trevisano heads, drain on paper towels, and cut in half lengthwise, removing outer leaves if necessary.

2 │ Heat olive oil and sauté trevisano until lightly browned (about 3–4 minutes each side over medium heat). Add pine nuts, balsamic vinegar, and honey.

3 │ Keep cooking trevisano until golden-brown on all sides. Season with salt and pepper, and serve at once as a hot appetizer.

➤ Side dish: Crusty bread for dipping in extra sauce
➤ Beverage: Not-too-dry white wine (e.g., Frascati)

TIP Trevisano is related to radicchio but is more tender and less bitter. Unfortunately, it's hard to find. But, this recipe is also excellent made with red Belgian endive, radicchio, or any type of chicory.

Easy │ For a Buffet

Spinach and Pine Nuts
Spinaci ai pinoli

SERVES 4:

➤ 1 lb young spinach leaves
Freshly grated nutmeg
3 cloves garlic
3 tbs pine nuts
2 tbs fresh lemon juice
1 pinch sugar
1/3 cup olive oil
Salt and pepper

🕐 Prep time: 25 minutes
➤ Calories per serving: About 235

1 │ Rinse spinach thoroughly, do not drain, and place in a pot. Add a little salt and nutmeg. Peel garlic, slightly crush cloves, and add. Cover and heat until the lid is too hot to touch. Reduce heat, keep covered, and continue cooking for 5 minutes. Drain in a colander and let cool slightly.

2 │ In a dry pan, toast pine nuts over low heat while stirring until golden-brown. Make a light sauce by mixing fresh lemon juice, 1 pinch salt, sugar, pepper, and olive oil. Pour spinach into a shallow dish, remove garlic cloves, drizzle with sauce, and sprinkle with pine nuts to serve.

➤ Serve warm as a side dish with sautéed meat or fish, or cold as part of an antipasti buffet
➤ Beverage: Velvety red wine (e.g., Dolcetto)

Specialty of Florence

Bread Salad
Panzanella

SERVES 4:

➤ 4 slices stale Italian bread

3 cloves garlic

2 small zucchini

$1/3$ cup olive oil for frying

1 small head romaine lettuce

2 yellow bell peppers

4 tomatoes (about 1 lb)

1 red onion

2 tbs white balsamic vinegar

$1/4$ cup olive oil for dressing

Salt and pepper

🕐 Prep time: 30 minutes

➤ Calories per serving: About 415

1 | Cut bread into cubes. Peel garlic. Rinse zucchini, pat dry, and slice. In a non-stick pan, heat 3 tbs of olive oil and toast bread and 1 crushed garlic clove until bread is golden; remove. Next, fry zucchini and 1 garlic clove in 2 tbs of olive oil until golden. Salt and pepper to taste; let cool slightly.

2 | Rinse lettuce and cut into bite-size strips. Rinse bell peppers and cut usable parts into small diamonds. Rinse tomatoes and cut into eighths. Peel onion, halve, and cut into thin wedges.

3 | For the dressing, combine vinegar, salt, freshly ground pepper, and olive oil. Rub the inside of a salad bowl with 1 garlic clove cut in half. Add all ingredients and gently toss with dressing. Serve immediately.

Easy | For Company

Arugula and Parmesan
Insalata di rucola

SERVES 4:

➤ 4 cups fresh arugula leaves

$1/4$ cup pine nuts

2 oz chunk Parmesan

2 small shallots

2 tbs balsamic vinegar

$1/4$ cup olive oil

$1/2$ lb cherry tomatoes

Salt and pepper

🕐 Prep time: 15 minutes

➤ Calories per serving: About 250

1 | Rinse arugula and drain well. In a dry pan, toast pine nuts over low heat until golden and let cool.

2 | Peel shallots and chop finely. Combine vinegar, shallots, salt, pepper, and olive oil for the dressing.

3 | Tear arugula into bite-size pieces and arrange on four plates. Rinse cherry tomatoes, halve, and place on arugula. With a vegetable peeler, shave Parmesan onto the salads. Drizzle on dressing and sprinkle with pine nuts.

➤ Variations: Add prosciutto or sautéed shrimp to transform this appetizer into a light evening meal.

➤ In place of Parmesan and pine nuts, try it with Gorgonzola and walnuts.

➤ Side dish: Ciabatta bread

➤ Beverage: White wine (e.g., Pinot Grigio)

Can Prepare in Advance

Seafood Salad
Antipasto di mare

SERVES 8:

➤ 2 lbs mixed seafood without shells (fresh or frozen)

$1/4$ cup olive oil for sautéeing

$1/2$ cup dry white wine (may substitute with water and 2 tbs fresh lemon juice)

$3/4$ cup parsley sprigs

4 cloves garlic

3 tbs fresh lemon juice

$1/3$ cup extra virgin olive oil

Salt and pepper

⏱ Prep time: 20 minutes

⏱ Marinating time: 2 hours

➤ Calories per serving: About 145

1 | Rinse seafood and drain or thaw. In a pan, heat about $1/4$ cup olive oil and sauté seafood until lightly browned. After 2 minutes, add white wine, cover, and stew over medium heat for about 5 minutes.

2 | For the dressing, rinse parsley and chop finely. Peel garlic and slice thinly. Combine fresh lemon juice, salt, pepper, parsley, garlic, and $1/3$ cup extra virgin olive oil.

3 | Season seafood with salt and pepper; let cool to lukewarm. Toss with dressing and refrigerate for at least 2 hours before serving.

TIP More and more, prepared seafood mixtures contain surimi, which are low-quality, pressed fish scraps that are processed and less than desirable. So, either remove the surimi or create your own seafood mixes by purchasing shrimp, squid, and other ingredients separately.

Easy

Artichokes
Carciofi alla casalinga

SERVES 4:

➤ 4 large artichokes

1 head garlic

$1/4$ cup olive oil

Salt and pepper

⏱ Prep time: 45 minutes

➤ Calories per serving: About 115

1 | Rinse artichokes and remove hard tips of leaves with kitchen scissors. Cut off stems close to the base. Separate garlic cloves, peel, spread open artichoke leaves and insert garlic cloves inside (halve cloves if necessary).

2 | In a pot (the appropriate size to fit the 4 artichokes), bring about 2 inches of salted water to a boil in the bottom. Place artichokes in water, season generously with salt and pepper, and drizzle each artichoke with 1 tbs olive oil. Cover and cook over medium heat for 40–45 minutes until the leaves are easy to detach.

TIP Garlic Dip

In a blender, blend 2 egg yolks, 1 tsp mustard, a little salt, and 1 tbs fresh lemon juice for 2 minutes. Very gradually blend in $1/2$ cup olive oil until you have a creamy mayonnaise. Fold in 3 garlic cloves squeezed through a press, 2 tbs chopped parsley, $1/3$ cup crème fraîche, salt, and pepper. Refrigerate until serving. (Do not serve raw egg products to the very young, elderly, or those with compromised immune systems. Consume raw egg products at your own risk.)

Photo top: **Seafood Salad** *Photo bottom:* **Artichokes** ➤

Primi Piatti: Pasta, Gnocchi, and Risotto

Where would Italian cuisine be without its pasta and rice dishes? These foods have long held a favorite spot on global menus. Whether served with a tomato sauce or cream sauce, vegetarian-style or with fish or meat, the possibilities are endless. This chapter's recipes are designed as a first course for 5–6 people. Served with a mixed salad, they can function as a main dish for 4 people.

Quick Recipes

Garlic Spaghetti
Spaghetti aglio e olio

SERVES 4:

➤ 1 lb spaghetti | 8 cloves garlic | 2 fresh red Fresno chiles (or crushed red pepper flakes) | 2 stalks parsley | $1/2$ cup olive oil | Salt and pepper

1 | In a large amount of salted water, cook spaghetti for 10 minutes or until al dente; drain. Peel garlic and mince. Finely chop usable parts of chile and parsley.

2 | In a large pan, heat olive oil. Sauté garlic and chile briefly. Add cooked spaghetti and parsley; toss briefly. Season with salt and pepper.

Lemon Pasta
Linguine al limone

SERVES 4:

➤ 1 lb linguine (may substitute tagliatelle) | 5 oz mascarpone (about $1/3$ cup) | $1/4$ cup fresh lemon juice and 2 tsp lemon zest | $3^1/2$ oz freshly grated Parmesan | $1/4$ cup fresh sprigs lemon balm | Salt and pepper

1 | Cook linguine in salted water for about 8 minutes or until al dente. In a prewarmed bowl, combine mascarpone, fresh lemon juice, lemon zest, and Parmesan. Season generously to taste with salt and pepper.

2 | Drain pasta and toss immediately with mascarpone-lemon mixture. Cut lemon balm into strips and add; fold together.

25

Child's Play
Tortellini "Aurora"

SERVES 4:

➤ Salt

1 (14 oz) can diced tomatoes

1 scant cup cream

1 clove garlic

Cayenne pepper

3/4 cup fresh basil sprigs

1 lb tortellini (any filling)

Parmesan for sprinkling

🕐 Prep time: 15 minutes

➤ Calories per serving: About 460

1 | Bring salted water to a boil for tortellini. Meanwhile, heat tomatoes (drained) and cream in a large pan and reduce over medium heat until thick and creamy. Peel garlic, squeeze through a press, and add. Season to taste with salt and cayenne. Rinse basil and cut leaves into fine strips.

2 | Cook tortellini in boiling water until they all float to the top, then drain. Add to tomato-cream sauce, sprinkle with basil, and toss. Serve at once, with Parmesan.

➤ Beverage: Red wine (e.g., Chianti)

Traditional
Rigatoni with Broccoli and Gorgonzola
Rigatoni con broccoli e gorgonzola

SERVES 4:

➤ 1 lb broccoli

1 lemon

1 onion

2 cloves garlic

2 tbs butter

5 oz Gorgonzola

2/3 cup cream

1 lb rigatoni

Salt and white pepper

Nutmeg

🕐 Prep time: 30 minutes

➤ Calories per serving: About 800

1 | Divide broccoli into florets and rinse. Rinse lemon, pat dry, and cut into thick slices. Bring salted water to a boil and cook broccoli and lemon slices at a rolling boil for 5 minutes. Drain and remove lemon slices.

2 | Bring water to a boil for the rigatoni. Meanwhile, peel onion and garlic; chop both finely. In a large pan, melt butter and sauté onion and garlic until translucent. Dice Gorgonzola coarsely and add along with cream to pan.

3 | Separately, place pasta in boiling, salted water and cook for 10–12 minutes or until al dente. Meanwhile, simmer Gorgonzola-cream mixture until it forms a creamy sauce. Heat broccoli in this mixture. Season generously to taste with salt, pepper, and nutmeg. Drain rigatoni and toss with sauce.

➤ Variation: If desired, add prosciutto strips (as pictured). You can also replace broccoli with spinach.

Photo top: **Tortellini "Aurora"**   *Photo bottom:* **Rigatoni with Broccoli and Gorgonzola** ➤

Vegetarian | For Company

Farfalle with Zucchini
Farfalle con zucchini

SERVES 4:

➤ 1 onion
1 lb zucchini
1 cup walnuts
1 lb farfalle pasta (bow tie shape)
2 tbs butter
1 scant cup cream
Salt
Cayenne pepper
Nutmeg

⊙ Prep time: 25 minutes
➤ Calories per serving: About 760

1 | Peel onion and dice finely. Rinse zucchini, trim ends, slice lengthwise, then cut slices crosswise into matchsticks. Chop walnuts coarsely.

2 | In a large pot, bring salted water to a boil. Add pasta and cook for about 10 minutes or until al dente. Meanwhile, melt butter in a large pan and sauté onion until translucent. Add zucchini and sauté over medium heat for 3–5 minutes. Add cream and season with salt, cayenne, and nutmeg. Reduce by cooking for 5 minutes or until creamy.

3 | Drain pasta, toss with sauce, and sprinkle with walnuts.

➤ Beverage: Light white wine (e.g., Frascati)

Spicy | Inexpensive

Penne with Tomato Sauce
Penne all'arrabbiata

SERVES 4:

➤ 1 onion
2 fresh red Fresno chiles
¼ cup olive oil
2 (14 oz) cans diced tomatoes
2 cloves garlic
2 ripe tomatoes
1 lb penne rigate
½ cup fresh basil sprigs
Salt

⊙ Prep time: 30 minutes
➤ Calories per serving: About 535

1 | Peel and chop onion. Finely chop red chiles. In a pot, heat oil and sauté onion until translucent. Add tomatoes and chiles, cover, and cook over medium heat for 10 minutes. Stir occasionally, until thick and creamy (cook uncovered if necessary). Peel garlic, squeeze through a press, and add. Simmer another 10 minutes.

2 | Meanwhile, bring a pot of salted water to a boil. Submerge fresh tomatoes into boiling water, peel, remove/discard seeds, and dice finely. Add to tomato sauce and season with salt. Cook penne pasta in the boiling salted water for about 10 minutes or until al dente. Rinse basil and cut into narrow strips.

3 | Transfer penne to plates, top each serving with some tomato sauce, and garnish with basil.

➤ Beverage: Hearty red wine (e.g., Chianti) or beer

Photo top: **Farfalle with Zucchini** Photo bottom: **Penne with Tomato Sauce** ➤

Easy | For Company

Orecchiette with Tuna
Orecchiette al tonno

SERVES 4:

- ➤ 1 onion
  7 oz canned oil-packed tuna
  1 lb orecchiette pasta
  ¼ cup olive oil
  1 (14 oz) can diced tomatoes
  1 cup fresh parsley sprigs
  1 tsp dried thyme
  ¼ cup rinsed capers
  Salt and pepper

- ⏱ Prep time: 20 minutes
- ➤ Calories per serving: About 620

1 | Bring salted water to a boil for the pasta. Peel onions and chop. Drain tuna. Cook orecchiette in boiling water for about 12 minutes or until al dente.

2 | In the meantime, heat olive oil in a large pan and sauté onions. Shred tuna with a fork and add. After 2 minutes, add tomatoes, cover, and let stew over medium heat. Rinse parsley and chop leaves finely. Season sauce with salt, pepper, and thyme. Add capers and continue stewing until the orecchiette is done.

3 | Drain pasta and toss with parsley and sauce. Serve without cheese.

Traditional

Gnocchi with Sage Butter
Gnocchi burro e salvia

SERVES 4:

- ➤ 1 lb fresh gnocchi (specialty store; refrigerated)
  3 sprigs sage
  2 oz (4 tbs) butter
  Salt and pepper
  Nutmeg
  Parmesan for sprinkling

- ⏱ Prep time: 10 minutes
- ➤ Calories per serving: About 245

1 | Bring salted water to a boil. Add fresh gnocchi and continue cooking in gently boiling water until they all float to the surface.

2 | Meanwhile, cut sage leaves in narrow strips. In a pan, melt butter but don't let it turn too brown. Add sage. Drain gnocchi and toss briefly with sage butter. Season with salt, pepper, and nutmeg. Serve sprinkled with grated or shaved Parmesan.

- ➤ Beverage: White wine (e.g., Pinot Grigio)

TIP

Making homemade gnocchi is fairly time-consuming so for quick cuisine, buy them ready-made. Gnocchi also pair well with the tomato cream sauce or Gorgonzola sauce on page 26.

Impressive

Saffron Risotto with Asparagus and Shrimp
Risotto al zafferano con asparagi e gamberetti

SERVES 4:

➤ ¹/₂ lb asparagus
2 shallots
3 cups vegetable stock
¹/₄ cup olive oil
1 generous cup risotto rice
Few threads saffron
³/₄ cup dry white wine
(may substitute vegetable stock)
¹/₂ lb peeled jumbo shrimp
3 oz (6 tbs) butter
Salt and white pepper

◷ Prep time: 30 minutes
Calories per serving:
About 610

1 | Peel bottom third of asparagus spears. Trim tough ends and cut remaining diagonally into 1-inch lengths. Peel shallots and mince. Heat vegetable stock.

2 | In a pot, heat oil and sauté shallots until translucent. Add rice and saffron threads and sauté over medium heat for 1 minute while stirring constantly. Pour in half the white wine.

3 | If the rice starts to dry out, pour in remaining wine and continue stirring. For the risotto to succeed, you must stir it constantly. Add a ladle of hot stock and stir. Each time the rice has soaked up the liquid, add 1 more ladleful of stock.

4 | After 10 minutes, add asparagus. After another 5 minutes, add jumbo shrimp.

5 | After a total of 20 minutes, begin testing the rice. The grains must still be firm but not hard. Cook for another couple minutes. When the risotto is done (i.e., the rice is tender but firm and has a creamy consistency but not too wet), fold in butter. Season to taste with salt and pepper and serve at once.

➤ Beverage: Dry white wine (e.g., Chardonnay)

TIP

A regional Italian rice, arborio, works especially well for risotto. The grains retain their firmness when cooked while offering up an enticing aroma.

Secondi piatti:
Fish and Meat

In Italy, the primo piatti serves to satisfy hunger and so is followed up by correspondingly small servings of meat and fish intended for pure enjoyment. Since that's not the customary American way, this book offers you a compromise solution—when served with a salad as an appetizer and a little fruit for dessert, the secondi piatti in this chapter are complete meals for 4 people. In a multi-course meal, they make enough to serve 5–6.

Quick Recipes

Pork Cutlets with Balsamic Vinegar
Scaloppine al balsamico

SERVES 4:

➤ 4 thin pork cutlets | 1 tbs flour | 1 clove garlic | ¼ cup olive oil | ⅓ cup balsamic vinegar | Salt and pepper

1 | Pound cutlets flat, season with salt and pepper, and dredge in flour. Peel garlic and crush slightly with a knife blade.

2 | In a pan, heat oil and add garlic. Fry cutlets for 3 minutes on each side and remove. Add balsamic vinegar to meat juice and heat briefly. Remove garlic cloves. Toss cutlets in balsamic vinegar sauce to serve.

Fried Shrimp
Scampi

SERVES 4:

➤ 16 shell-on jumbo shrimp | 5 cloves garlic | 1 cup fresh parsley sprigs | 1 lemon | ⅓ cup olive oil | Salt and pepper

1 | Without peeling, halve shrimp lengthwise using a sharp knife (serrated works well). Peel garlic, rinse parsley, and finely chop both. Squeeze juice from lemon.

2 | In two large pans, heat olive oil and sauté shrimp halves for 2 minutes. Add garlic and parsley and toss with shrimp. Season with salt and pepper and drizzle with lemon juice. Sauté for another 3 minutes.

Easy

Pan-Fried Squid
Calamari in padella

SERVES 4:

➤ 2 lbs cleaned squid fillets and tentacles

1 bunch spring garlic or wild garlic (may substitute green onions)

$1/3$ cup olive oil

$1/3$ cup white wine (may substitute with water and 2 tbs lemon juice)

Salt and pepper

🕐 Prep time: 25 minutes

➤ Calories per serving: About 380

1 | Rinse squid and cut tentacles into pieces and bodies into rings. Rinse wild garlic and cut coarsely into strips.

2 | In a pan, heat oil and sauté squid over medium heat. After 2 minutes, add white wine and season with salt and pepper. Cover and stew for another 2 minutes. Add wild garlic and toss briefly.

➤ Beverage: Sparkling white wine (e.g., Prosecco, Verdicchio)

TIP
Wild garlic is available only in the spring from specialty growers. You can substitute 2 cloves garlic and 1 bunch parsley.

Traditional | For Company

Mussels in Tomato Sauce
Cozze al pomodoro

SERVES 4:

➤ 4 lbs mussels

1 large onion

4 cloves garlic

1 fresh red Fresno chile

$1/3$ cup olive oil

2 (14 oz) cans diced tomatoes

1 cup fresh parsley sprigs

Salt and pepper

🕐 Prep time: 30 minutes

➤ Calories per serving: About 315

1 | Rinse mussels and pull off beards if present. Discard any open mussels. Peel onion and garlic. Finely chop onion, garlic, and chile. In a large pot, heat olive oil and sauté onion, garlic, and chile. Add tomatoes and season generously with salt and pepper. Rinse parsley and chop leaves.

2 | Add mussels to pot, cover and cook for about 8 minutes until mussels open, vigorously shaking the pot from time to time.

3 | At this point, discard any closed mussels, which may be spoiled. Distribute remaining mussels on plates and sprinkle with parsley. Provide an empty plate for mussel shells when serving.

➤ Side dish: Crusty bread for dipping in the extra sauce

➤ Beverage: White wine (e.g., Pinot Bianco)

Photo top: **Pan-Fried Squid**   *Photo bottom:* **Mussels in Tomato Sauce** ➤

For Company | Impressive

Monkfish Medallions with Vegetable Gratin
Coda di rospo con gratin di patate, zucchini e pomodori

SERVES 4:

➤ **For the gratin:**

2 zucchini (about ³/₄ lb)

¹/₂ lb small tomatoes on the vine

1 lb firm potatoes (e.g., fingerlings)

2 sprigs fresh thyme

¹/₃ cup olive oil

2 oz grated Parmesan

Salt and pepper

➤ **For the fish:**

8 monkfish medallions (about 3 oz each)

3 tbs fresh lemon juice

¹/₃ cup olive oil

Salt and pepper

⏱ Prep time: 1 hour

➤ Calories per serving: About 515

1 | For the gratin, rinse zucchini and tomatoes, trim unusable parts, and slice remaining. Peel potatoes and cut into thin slices. Season all three ingredients with salt and pepper. Strip off thyme leaves and sprinkle over prepared vegetables. Preheat oven to 350°F.

2 | Brush a casserole dish with a little olive oil and alternately arrange potato, zucchini, and tomato slices tightly together and on end. Drizzle with olive oil and bake (middle rack) for 30 minutes.

3 | Rinse monkfish medallions and pat dry with paper towels. Salt and drizzle with lemon juice on both sides.

4 | Sprinkle grated Parmesan on the gratin in the oven and bake another 10 minutes until a golden crust forms.

5 | Meanwhile, heat oil in a pan and sauté monkfish medallions for 3 minutes on each side. Arrange on prewarmed plates with a serving of the gratin.

➤ Variation: Not quite authentic but tasty— season monkfish medallions with salt and lemon pepper and mix pan juices with freshly squeezed orange juice. To bind the sauce, whisk in ice-cold butter (or thicken with a cornstarch-cold water mixture).

➤ Beverage: Elegant white wine (e.g., Chardonnay)

Traditional

Veal Escalopes with Sage
Saltimbocca alla romana

SERVES 4:

- 8 thin veal escalopes (about 3 oz each)

  8 sage leaves

  4 slices prosciutto di Parma

  2 oz (4 tbs) cold butter

  $1/4$ cup olive oil

  $1/2$ cup dry Marsala (may substitute white wine or veal stock)

  Salt and pepper

  Wooden toothpicks

- Prep time: 25 minutes
- Calories per serving: About 570

1 | Season escalopes on both sides with salt and pepper. Top each with a half slice prosciutto and 1 sage leaf; secure with 1 toothpick. Dice butter and place in freezer.

2 | In a pan, heat oil and sauté escalopes for 3 minutes on each side, until golden. Remove from pan and keep warm on a plate covered with saran wrap.

3 | Pour leftover oil out of pan, but do not scrape or clean the pan. Reheat pan, add Marsala, and simmer while stirring to loosen pan juices. Using a wire whisk, stir ice cold butter into sauce but don't let it boil. Arrange 2 escalopes on each plate and top with sauce.

- Side dishes: Saffron rice and buttered vegetables

Also Delicious Cold

Veal Rolls
Involtini

SERVES 4:

- 2 green onions

  $1/2$ lb fresh spinach

  8 thin veal escalopes (about 4 oz each)

  $1/2$ cup ricotta

  $1/3$ cup olive oil

  $1/2$ cup white wine (may substitute stock)

  $1/2$ cup veal stock (or beef broth)

  Salt and pepper

  Wooden toothpicks

- Prep time: 45 minutes
- Calories per serving: About 425

1 | Rinse green onions, trim ends, and chop usable parts into fine rings. Rinse spinach thoroughly and remove stems. Place wet spinach in a pot, cover, heat, and let wilt for 5 minutes. Drain and let cool, then squeeze out liquid, and spread out on paper towels.

2 | Season escalopes on both sides with salt and pepper. Coat each slice with a thin layer of ricotta (leaving a $1/2$-inch border with no ricotta), top with spinach and green onions; season with salt and pepper. Roll up involtini and secure with toothpicks.

3 | In a large pan, heat olive oil and fry involtini on all sides until golden. Pour in wine, cover, and stew over medium heat for 10 minutes. Add veal stock and simmer for another 10 minutes.

- Variation: The involtini also taste great with a pesto filling (see cover photo and recipes for pesto on page 11).

Photo top: **Veal Escalopes with Sage**   *Photo bottom:* **Veal Rolls**

For Company | Also Delicious Cold

Lemon-Thyme Chicken
Pollo al timo e limone

SERVES 4:

- 1 large fryer chicken (about 3 lbs)
  1 bunch thyme
  2 lemons
  $1/3$ cup olive oil
  1 cup dry white wine (may substitute chicken stock)
  Salt and pepper

- Prep time: 1 hour
- Calories per serving: About 625

1 | Cut chicken into 8 pieces. Break off small sprigs of thyme and insert under chicken skin. Season chicken pieces with salt and pepper. Rinse lemons and cut into eighths, removing any seeds.

2 | Preheat oven to 350°F. In a roasting pan, heat olive oil and sauté meat on all sides until lightly browned. Add lemon pieces and remaining thyme sprigs and let cook briefly. Pour in white wine.

3 | Transfer chicken to oven (middle rack); bake for 25 minutes or until cooked through. (If the liquid cooks down too much, add a little water.) Ready to serve.

- Variation: This roasted chicken also tastes great with rosemary and young garlic.
- Side dish: Vegetable rice
- Beverage: White wine (e.g., Chardonnay)

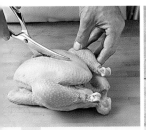

1 Cut in half
Use poultry shears to cut chicken in half.

2 Cut in pieces
Cut off thighs and wings and separate breast sides.

3 Season
Pull skin away from the meat and insert thyme.

4 Brown
Brown chicken pieces and then add lemon pieces.

Specialty of Liguria | For Special Occasions

Rabbit with Pine Nuts and Olives
Coniglio con pinoli e olive

SERVES 4:

➤ **1 rabbit (about 3 lbs)**
   1 onion
   2 cloves garlic
   $1/2$ cup olive oil
   $2/3$ cup pine nuts
   3 sprigs fresh herbs (e.g., sage, rosemary, lavender)
   1 bay leaf
   1 cup dry white wine (may substitute stock)
   1 cup veal stock (or beef broth)
   1 cup imported black olives (e.g., kalamata, Niçoise)
   Salt and pepper

⏱ Prep time: 1 hour
➤ Calories per serving: About 875

1 | Cut rabbit into 6–8 pieces (or have butcher do this) and season with salt and pepper. Peel onion and garlic; chop both finely. Preheat oven to 350°F.

2 | In a roasting pan, heat olive oil and sauté rabbit pieces on all sides until lightly browned. Add onion, garlic, and pine nuts and sauté briefly. Add herb sprigs and bay leaf. Pour in wine.

3 | Transfer rabbit to oven (middle rack) and bake for 20 minutes. Turn over rabbit pieces, pour in a little stock and bake 15 more minutes. Finally, add olives and remaining stock; cook for 15 minutes or until cooked throughout.

➤ Side dish: Oven-roasted vegetables or simply a piece of focaccia (Italian flatbread)
➤ Beverage: White wine (e.g., Trebbiano)

TIP

Variation with potatoes

Instead of olives and pine nuts, use 1 lb firm potatoes, $1/2$ lb cherry tomatoes, and twice the amount of veal stock. Prepare and brown rabbit as described. Add chopped onions, garlic, and herb sprigs (rosemary and thyme are best), add white wine, and transfer to 350°F oven. After 20 minutes, peel potatoes and cut into quarters or eighths depending on size. Add and roast along with rabbit for 20 minutes. Then, add veal stock at regular intervals—the potatoes soak up the sauce while roasting. At the end, add cherry tomatoes and roast for 5 minutes until tender. Season pan juices with salt and black pepper to taste. Instead of drinking white wine, this pairs well with a young red wine (e.g., Merlot).

Easy | For Company

Pork Fillet with Salsa Verde and Rosemary Potatoes

Filetto di maiale con salsa verde e patate al rosmarino

SERVES 4:

➤ 2 lbs firm potatoes

4 sprigs rosemary

1/3 cup olive oil

1 1/2 lbs pork tenderloin
(from thickest part)

2 cloves garlic

Salt and pepper

➤ For the salsa verde:

2 cups mixed herb leaves
(e.g., basil, tarragon,
chervil, parsley)

2 green onions

3 tbs white wine vinegar

1 clove garlic

1/3 cup olive oil

Salt and pepper

⏲ Prep time: 1 hour

➤ Calories per serving:
About 585

1 | Preheat oven to 350°F. Peel potatoes, cut into quarters or eighths depending on size, and spread out on a baking sheet. Strip rosemary needles from 2 sprigs and sprinkle over potatoes. Drizzle with 4 tbs of the olive oil; bake (middle rack), turning occasionally.

2 | Meanwhile, season pork on all sides with salt and pepper. In a pan, heat remaining olive oil and brown meat on all sides over medium heat. Peel garlic, crush slightly, and add. Add 2 remaining rosemary sprigs. When pork is browned on all sides, remove from pan and wrap in aluminum foil along with herb sprigs and garlic. Push rosemary potatoes to one side and place pork (in foil) on the baking sheet. Bake for about 12 more minutes.

3 | Meanwhile, make the salsa verde: Rinse herbs and green onions; mince all finely. Combine herbs and green onions with salt, pepper, and white wine vinegar. Peel garlic, squeeze through a press, and add. Add olive oil, whisking.

4 | Test the meat for doneness: As soon as it feels firm (i.e., is no longer soft and yielding when you press down on it with your finger), it is done even though it's still pink in the middle. If you don't like it pink, leave it in the oven for 5 more minutes. Or, test with a meat thermometer and make sure it registers 160°F.

5 | Remove pork from oven but keep sealed in foil for 10 minutes; then slice. Salt potatoes and serve with meat and salsa verde.

➤ Beverage: Hearty red wine (e.g., Nobile di Montepulciano)

TIP The salsa verde keeps longer if you add more oil.

46

Fancy | For Gourmets

Lamb Chops with Balsamic Vinegar Potatoes
Costolette di agnello con patate al aceto balsamico

SERVES 4:

➤ 1¼ lbs very small new potatoes

1 egg

2 tbs breadcrumbs

2 tbs freshly grated Parmesan

2 tbs chopped herbs (e.g., thyme, rosemary, and parsley)

12 frenched lamb chops (about 2 oz each)

⅓ cup olive oil

¾ cup fresh basil sprigs

¼ cup balsamic vinegar

2 tbs honey

Salt and pepper

🕐 Prep time: 50 minutes

➤ Calories per serving: About 955

1 | Rinse potatoes and boil with the peels on for about 20 minutes. Let cool.

2 | Beat egg in a shallow bowl with 1 tbs cold water. In a second bowl, combine bread-crumbs, Parmesan, and herbs. Season lamb chops with salt and pepper. Dip each chop briefly in egg and dredge in bread-crumb mixture.

3 | In a large pan, heat 4 tbs of the olive oil and fry potatoes on all sides until crispy and brown.

4 | Meanwhile, in another pan, heat 3 tbs olive oil and fry lamb chops for about 3 minutes on each side until lightly browned. Keep cooked lamb chops warm in a 170°F oven.

5 | Rinse basil and cut leaves into fine strips. Just before serving, add balsamic vinegar, honey, and basil strips to potatoes; toss and season with salt and pepper.

➤ Beverage: Sophisticated red wine (e.g., Barolo)

TIP

You can serve this combination of lamb chops with balsamic vinegar potatoes along with the arugula salad on page 20 or with tender green beans as follows:

For the beans: To serve 4 people, rinse 1 lb beans and trim ends. Cook in boiling, salted water for 4–5 minutes or until al dente; plunge immediately into ice-cold water so they will retain their bright color. Finely chop 2 shallots and sauté in 2 tbs olive oil until translucent. Add green beans to pan to reheat, tossing. Season with salt, pepper, and a little chopped thyme.

Dolci e formaggi:
Sweet Desserts and Cheese

No meal is complete without a delectable dessert. Those who have a real sweet tooth consider it even more important than the main course! Be sure to also try cheese course combinations like the Fanned Pears with Gorgonzola or the Piquant Ricotta Cream.

Quick Recipes

Watermelon with Grappa
Cocomero alla grappa

SERVES 12:

➤ 1 cup Grappa | 1 watermelon (about 8 lbs) | Disposable syringe (pharmacy or grilling store)

1 | Fill syringe with Grappa and inject alcohol into the melon on all sides. Let stand in the refrigerator for at least 2 hours (or refrigerate overnight).

2 | To serve, cut into wedges and arrange on a large platter.

Cheese and Fruit Platter
Formaggi con frutta

SERVES 10:

➤ 1$^1\!/_2$ lbs various cheeses (e.g., Gorgonzola, Taleggio, Scamorza, Pecorino, Parmesan) | 1 lb grapes | 5 fresh figs | Walnut halves, pistachios, and toasted almonds

1 | Arrange pieces of cheese on a platter. Rinse fruit and arrange between cheese pieces. It's best to cut figs in quarters. Sprinkle nuts in between and serve with nut bread or ciabatta.

2 | Make sure to take cheese(s) out of the refrigerator 30 minutes before serving.

For Company | Fruity

Mascarpone Cream with Strawberries
Crema di mascarpone con fragole

SERVES 4:

- 1 lb strawberries
  3 tbs sugar
  3 tbs orange liqueur (may substitute 2 tbs fresh lemon juice)
  1/2 cup cream
  2 very fresh egg yolks
  8 oz mascarpone

- Prep time: 25 minutes
- Calories per serving: About 490

1 | Rinse strawberries and set aside half the strawberries for garnish. Remove stems from and dice the rest; marinate with 1 tbs of the sugar and the orange liqueur.

2 | Beat cream until stiff peaks form. In a separate mixing bowl, beat egg yolks and the remaining 2 tbs sugar into a foamy, white cream. Stir in mascarpone. Fold in marinated strawberry pieces and whipped cream.

3 | Transfer mascarpone cream to four dessert bowls and garnish with remaining strawberries (halved or whole).
Note: Do not serve raw egg to children, the elderly, or anyone with a compromised immune system.

> **TIP**
>
> **Orange liqueur**
>
> For desserts, you can use any of the following three orange-flavored liqueurs: Triple Sec, Cointreau, or Grand Marnier

Can Prepare in Advance | For Company

Panna Cotta with Raspberries
Panna cotta con lamponi

FILLS 4 SMALL DESSERT MOLDS (2/3 CUP EACH):

- 6 leaves white gelatin (specialty baking store)
  1 scant cup cream
  1 1/4 cups whole milk
  1/4 cup sugar
  1 vanilla bean
  1/2 lb raspberries
  2 tsp chopped pistachios

- Prep time: 25 minutes
- Refrigeration time: 4 hours
- Calories per serving: About 280

1 | Soften gelatin in cold water for 10 minutes. In a pot, heat cream, milk, and sugar. Slit open vanilla bean lengthwise, scrape out pulp, and add. Bring to a boil and immediately remove from heat. Using a wire whisk, dissolve gelatin completely into cream-milk mixture. Pour panna cotta into four dessert molds and refrigerate for 4 hours.

2 | Sort raspberries. Unmold panna cotta by running the blade of a sharp knife around the edges, briefly submerging ramekin bottoms in hot water, and then reversing onto dessert plates. Surround with fresh raspberries and sprinkle with pistachios.

Fancy | For Company

Peach Gratin
Pesche gratinate

FILLS 4 SHALLOW,
INDIVIDUAL GRATIN DISHES:

➤ 4 ripe peaches (about 1 lb)
  2 tbs fresh lemon juice
  2 eggs
  2 tbs sugar
  3 tbs Amaretto (optional)
  2 tsp toasted, slivered almonds
  Butter for greasing dishes

🕐 Prep time: 30 minutes
➤ Calories per serving:
  About 195

1 | Grease gratin dishes with a little butter. Preheat oven to 425°F.

2 | Submerge peaches briefly in boiling water, peel, halve, and remove pits. Cut fruit into narrow wedges and arrange in greased gratin or baking dishes in a fan pattern. Drizzle with a little fresh lemon juice to keep the peaches from turning brown.

3 | Separate eggs and beat whites until very stiff peaks form. In another bowl, beat egg yolks and sugar into a foamy white cream. Add Amaretto and then fold this mixture into the stiff egg whites. Distribute mixture on peaches and bake (middle rack) for 10–12 minutes. When the surface starts to brown, remove peaches from oven, sprinkle with slivered almonds and serve while warm.

Traditional |
For Gourmets

Figs in Red Wine
Fichi al vino rosso

SERVES 4:

➤ 12 fresh figs
  1 cup hearty red wine (e.g., Barolo)
  3 tbs sugar
  1/2 vanilla bean
  1 stick cinnamon

🕐 Prep time: 15 minutes
🕐 Refrigeration time: 4 hours
➤ Calories per serving:
  About 180

1 | Rinse figs thoroughly and pat dry with paper towels. Without peeling, cut into quarters, remove any hard stems, and place in a bowl.

2 | Combine red wine, sugar, half vanilla bean (slit open lengthwise), and cinnamon stick; heat but don't let boil. Pour over figs and let cool; cover and refrigerate for 4 hours.

3 | To serve, remove vanilla bean and cinnamon stick. Transfer figs and wine to four goblets and serve with Italian almond cookies (Cantucci).

➤ Variation: These figs are also excellent in Vin Santo. In this case, omit all or part of the sugar.

Impressive | Can
Prepare in Advance

Fanned Pears with Gorgonzola
Pere con gorgonzola

SERVES 4:

- ➤ ³/₄ cup walnut halves
  - ¹/₃ lb gorgonzola
  - 2 tbs mascarpone
  - Black pepper
  - 4 ripe pears

- ⏲ Prep time: 20 minutes
- ➤ Calories per serving: About 330

1 | Coarsely chop all but 12 walnut halves. Mash gorgonzola with a fork, stir together with mascarpone, and fold in chopped walnuts. Season with black pepper and refrigerate.

2 | Just before serving, peel pears, cut in half, and carefully cut out cores. Starting from the base, make multiple lengthwise cuts in pears and fan out 2 pear halves on each plate. Arrange 2 balls of Gorgonzola cream next to fanned pears and garnish with remaining walnuts.

- ➤ Side dish: Fresh nut bread
- ➤ Beverage: Follow up with Grappa

Can Prepare in Advance

Piquant Ricotta Cream
Crema di ricotta

SERVES 4:

- ➤ ¹/₃ cup pine nuts
  - 6 sun-dried tomatoes (oil-packed)
  - 10 black imported olives (e.g., kalamata)
  - 4 fresh thyme sprigs
  - 8 oz ricotta
  - Salt and pepper

- ⏲ Prep time: 20 minutes
- ➤ Calories per serving: About 260

1 | In an ungreased pan, toast pine nuts until golden. Drain sun-dried tomatoes and dice finely. Remove pits from olives and dice finely. Chop thyme leaves finely.

2 | Place ricotta in a bowl and season with salt, pepper, and thyme. Carefully fold in sun-dried tomatoes, olives, and pine nuts. This goes especially well on freshly toasted Italian bread or olive bread.

TIP

Ricotta cream makes an ideal crostini spread with an aperitif and can also be used as an everyday vegetarian spread. It keeps easily for 1 week in the refrigerator, so it's worth it to make extra.

Photo top: **Fanned Pears with Gorgonzola**   *Photo bottom:* **Piquant Ricotta Cream** ➤

Whipping up a Multi-Course Meal

4 people – 30 minutes

Menu sequence

Arugula and Parmesan (page 20)
Pork Cutlets with Balsamic Vinegar and
    Ribbon Pasta (page 35)
Fresh fruit

You also need
1 lb ribbon pasta
Fresh fruit for dessert

What to do
1. Rinse and prepare fruit.
2. Prepare arugula salad.
3. Prepare pork cutlets.
4. Heat pasta water.
5. Eat salad.
6. Cook pasta while frying cutlets.
7. Serve main dish.
8. Serve fruit course.

4 people – 1 hour

Menu sequence

Melon and Prosciutto (page 13)
Farfalle with Zucchini (page 28)
Mascarpone Cream with Strawberries (page 52)

You also need
White crusty Italian bread
Freshly grated Parmesan

What to do
1. Prepare mascarpone cream dessert
   and refrigerate.
2. Rinse strawberries and set aside.
3. Prepare zucchini and onion; chop walnuts.
4. Arrange melon and prosciutto, serve with
   crusty white bread, and eat.
5. Boil pasta while making zucchini sauce.
6. Serve pasta and Parmesan.
7. Garnish Mascarpone cream with
   strawberries and serve.

Using This Book

4 people – 90 minutes

Menu sequence

Crostini with Arugula Pesto and Bresàola
(page 14) as aperitif
Artichokes with Garlic Dip (page 22)
Rabbit with Pine Nuts and Olives (page 44)
Fanned Pears with Gorgonzola (page 56)

You also need

Focaccia (Italian flatbread; may substitute
crusty white bread)

What to do

1. Prepare gorgonzola cream and refrigerate.
2. Make arugula pesto.
3. Prepare garlic dip.
4. Prepare artichokes.
5. Just before guests arrive, toast bread
for crostini.
6. Brown rabbit and place in hot oven; heat
artichokes on the stove.
7. Top crostini and eat as aperitif with guests.
8. Serve artichokes with dip, meanwhile
monitoring rabbit.
9. Serve rabbit and focaccia.
10. Arrange fanned pears with
gorgonzola cream.

8 People – 2 hours

Menu sequence

Tomato-Basil Toast (page 14) as aperitif
Lemon Pasta with Fried Shrimp (page 25,
$1/2$ serving per person)
Pork Fillet with Salsa Verde (page 46)
Cheese and Fruit Platter (page 51)
Watermelon with Grappa (page 51)

You also need

Double the ingredients for bruschetta and
pork fillet with side dishes
12 shrimp
Ciabatta and nut bread

What to do

1. Two hours ahead of time, prepare melon
and cheese platters and refrigerate.
2. Prepare salsa verde and bruschetta topping.
3. Just before guests arrive, prepare rosemary
potatoes; remove cheese from refrigerator.
4. Brown pork tenderloin and wrap in
aluminum foil.
5. Toast white bread and top with spread.
6. Place potatoes in hot oven.
7. Serve aperitif and bruschetta.
8. Prepare linguine; cut shrimp in half, sauté
in oil; place 3 halves on each serving of linguine.
9. Place pork tenderloin in hot oven.
10. Serve lemon pasta and shrimp.
11. Serve pork tenderloin with side dishes.
12. Serve cheese and nut bread and
then serve watermelon.

Using this Index

To help you find recipes containing certain ingredients more quickly, this index lists favorite ingredients (such as salmon and tomatoes) in bold type, followed by the corresponding recipes.

ABBREVIATIONS

lb = pound
oz = ounce
tsp = teaspoon
tbs = tablespoon

The Author

Margit Proebst, born in 1957, studied art history and philosophy in Munich meanwhile establishing a catering service and working as a food stylist. Her love of art—and of good food—regularly takes her on extended trips, through Italy, Spain, and France. She has been working as a cookbook author in Munich since 1999.

The Photographer

After completing his studies and assistantships, in 1992 **Michael Boyny** opened his own photography studio in Munich where he specializes in travel and food photography. The work he does for magazines and book publishers is a synthesis of these two key aspects of his career.

Photo Credits

FoodPhotographie Eising, Martina Görlach: cover photo
Stockfood: pages 3, 8, 9
Teubner Foodfoto: pages 4, 5
All others: Michael Boyny, Munich

Published originally under the title Italienische Blitz-menüs: Urlaubsgenuss im Handumdrehen © 2002 Gräfe und Unzer Verlag GmbH, Munich. English translation for the U.S. market © 2003, Silverback Books, Inc.

American food editor: Kelsey Lane
Managing editor: Birgit Rademacker
Editor: Tanja Dusy
Reader: Lynda Zuber Sassi and Adelheid Schmidt-Thomé
Typesetting and production: Patty Holden and Verlagsatz Lingner
Layout, typography, and cover design: Independent Medien Design, Munich
Production: Helmut Giersberg
Reproduction: Repro Schmidt, Dornbirn
Printing and binding: Druckhaus Kaufmann, Lahr

Printed in Singapore

ISBN 978-1-930603-67-7

Enjoy Other Quick & Easy Books

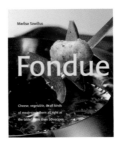

Marlisa Szwillus

Fondue

Cheese, vegetable, or all kinds of meat—cook them all right at the table in less than 50 recipes.

Cornelia Adam

Salads

An array of salads to eat as appetizers, entrées, and party dishes. Includes classic choices and cutting-edge alternatives.

Sandwiches

Xenia Burgdorf

Cornelia Adam

Quiche

Delicious, savory pies with vegetables, meat, poultry or fish—serve for all occasions.

Cornelia Adam

Garlic

Sophisticated Recipes with the Fantastic Spice of the Mediterranean Region Spicy (tangy), Fine (delicate), International

Cornelia Schinharl

Easy Vegetarian

Uncomplicated and sophisticated – Vegetarian recipes for all seasons

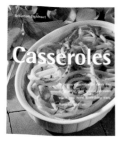

Sebastian Dickhaut

Casseroles

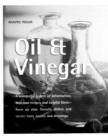

Annette Heisch

Oil & Vinegar

A wonderful source of information, delicious recipes and helpful hints— liven up your favorite dishes and create tasty sauces and dressings.

Andreas Fürtmayr

Sushi

Classic ideas from Japan and new fusion sushi Home-made perfectly

1 Noodle, 50 Sauces

Everyday Pasta • Old and New Italian Dishes Noodle biography • 10 Tips for Success

Healthy Wok

Elizabeth Doerge Christian Willrich Joern Rebbe

Great for light and satisfying meals

Antje Gruener

Grilling

Crisp, flavorful and fast—adaptable sources from the grill for your everyday feast, from spareribs to skewered vegetables with sauces and chutneys.

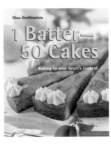

Gina Greifenstein

1 Batter— 50 Cakes

Baking to your heart's content

Cooking in Clay

Healthy Recipes with Great Flavor

Erika Casparek-Türkkan

Doris Muliar

Cocktails for Drivers

100% Enjoyment

Antipasti and Tapas

Mediterranean Appetizers Cornelia Schinharl

Soups

Classic to Contemporary

Sebastian Dickhaut

Claudia Schmidt

Raclette

New Recipes with Cheese Primer and Party Dips

THINGS TO HAVE ON HAND

- ➤ A variety of your favorite pasta types
- ➤ Canned, chopped tomatoes
- ➤ Garlic and olive oil
- ➤ A piece of fresh Parmesan
- ➤ Fresh herbs, salad ingredients, and fruit

Success for Fast Italian Meals

QUANTITIES FOR PASTA DISHES

- ➤ As appetizer for a 3- or 4-course meal: $2/3$ to $3/4$ cup dry pasta per person
- ➤ As entrée: 1 to $1\frac{1}{4}$ cups per person
- ➤ Gnocchi: 4 to 5 oz per person
- ➤ Risotto rice: $1/4$ to $1/3$ cup dry rice per person

SALAD DRESSINGS

- ➤ Mix salt and pepper and diced shallots or garlic into (preferably balsamic) vinegar until the salt dissolves.
- ➤ Add olive oil at the end and continue whisking until you have a creamy mixture.
- ➤ 2 parts vinegar to 5 parts oil

HERBS ON THE WINDOWSILL

- ➤ Rosemary, thyme, sage, oregano, and basil thrive in a sunny spot on the windowsill.
- ➤ Rosemary, thyme, and sage love to be dry. Basil needs lots of water every day.